CORY HARTMAN

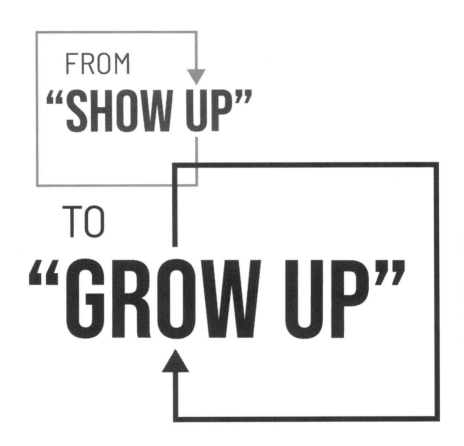

FROM "SHOW UP" TO "GROW UP"

How to Make Top Content That Makes Real Disciples

Cover design by Richard Fink.

ISBN-13: 9781071080276

CONTENTS

Part 1: The Church's Communication Problem

Part 2: The Church's Content Solution

Part 1

The Church's Communication Problem

1

SHOWING UP

The Gigantic Assumption behind 80-Plus Percent of Church Communication

"Showing up," Woody Allen famously said, "is 80 percent of life."

In the conventional wisdom of ministry, showing up is also 80 percent of church.

I'm not referring to *you* showing up—you do a lot more than that. *You* are working hard out of eyesight of everyone. *You* are responding to scores of emails. *You* are studying and praying and preparing and practicing for those moments when everyone *else* shows up.

That's the 80 percent I'm talking about: 80 percent of church is *other people* showing up. *Will my staff show up? Will my leaders show up? Will my volunteers show up? Will my people show up?*

And the most anxiety-producing question of all: *will NEW people show up?* Especially, will people who don't show up to any church, anywhere, show up?

Eighty percent of our anxieties, perhaps as much of our efforts, and in most cases nearly all of our outbound communication rest on this question.

However, if showing up really is 80 percent of church, then we are in bad shape today. We're getting failing marks on the assignment that constitutes 80 percent of our grade.

Why People Aren't Showing Up

Church attendance is declining all over North America. It's declining in small churches, medium-sized churches, and large churches. It's declining in rural, urban, and suburban churches. It's declining in long-established churches and newer churches. It's declining in liberal churches and conservative churches. It's declining in churches of every denomination. It's declining in churches of every ethnic background.

Showing up isn't declining in every single church, but it is declining in every single *kind* of church, nearly indiscriminately.

Carey Nieuwhof writes, "Every generation experiences change. But sometimes you sense you're in the midst of truly radical change, the kind that happens only every few centuries. Increasingly, I think we're in such a moment now."[1]

Setting aside outsiders (people not already connected to one's church) for a moment, insiders' shifting behavior alone has a lot to do with attendance decline. Simply put, participation frequency is decreasing. It's not that you're losing people; it's that your people are coming less often. "Regular attendance" used to mean attending worship about 50 Sundays a year. Now it may be half that, for a host of reasons.

We can blame affluence, travel, programmed youth activities outside the church, longer working hours that crowd out time to relax and time to go shopping and wash the car, and on and on. We might even credit a broad, healthy retreat from legalistic preaching and teaching that blows correct religious behaviors—including church attendance—out of proportion to the whole of the Christian life.

Yet there's also a spooky factor that is fed by all of these influences yet seems to be larger than all of them. It's that people want to show up less often, not just to church, but to anything. And increasingly, they don't have to.

People used to have to show up to a physical workplace to keep a job. Not anymore, depending on the profession and the organization.

People used to have to show up to a store to get possessions and supplies. Not anymore. (Thank you, Amazon.)

People used to have to show up to the theater to watch a good movie—or even to a video store to rent one. Not anymore. (Thank you, Netflix.)

People used to have to show up to a stadium to watch a college football game. Even though games have been televised for a long time, until recently many or even most of them were not. Now all of them are. (Thank you, ESPN.) Even as major college athletic programs are raking in money from TV rights at an unprecedented rate, aggregate attendance at football games has declined for the last four consecutive years for the first time in history.

I'm not rattling off these exhibits to set up an argument for "online church." That's a conversation (or debate) worth having, but it's not my subject here. My point is that, even aside from "the rise of the nones"[2]—which is hugely important to this dynamic—there are broad, complex, impersonal, all-encompassing economic and sociocultural influences on people both not to *have* to show up and not to *want* to show up . . . to anything.

The Communications Audit

So, the church is only one institution that's feeling the strain of this shift. But the church is feeling it especially intensely because of how much weight we've laid on showing up.

More importantly for this book, our communications, both inbound and outbound, revolve around it.

Try this tiny research project: a communications audit. Count up every discrete online message from your church that is visible to the general public over a modest period of time. It could be over the last 14 or 30 or 90 days, depending on how vigorous your church is at communicating. The audit encompasses your website, all your social media feeds, your YouTube or Vimeo channel, your podcast, and so on. And when I'm talking about a "discrete message," I mean every news item, post, tweet, article, episode, video.

Now, of those messages, what percentage was *not* either advertising an event you wanted people to show up to or photographically documenting an event that people already showed up to (or should have)?

Do you see where I'm going with this?

Now, from what remains, clear away any messages that require viewing or listening for more than seven minutes. (There go the sermons and podcast eps.) Then clear away the remaining messages that require a modest degree of Christian knowledge to understand them. What percentage of your total number of online messages do you have left?

That percentage is how much of your communication (1) addresses unchurched and barely churched people (2) that they could consume in a fairly short time (3) that *isn't* primarily trying to get them to show up.

All the rest either tries to get people to show up or else communicates a message to those already committed enough to the faith to understand the message and/or spend a hefty chunk of time consuming it.

For most churches, that "all the rest" adds up to more than Woody Allen's 80 percent.

What Are We Communicating For?

I hope you're beginning to see what I've begun to see—that the implicit purpose behind almost all church communication is to get people to show up . . . to our worship services, our outreach events, our small groups, our vision nights.

Now, I believe in showing up. I show up quite a bit myself. I'm raising my kids to show up, I invite unbelievers to show up, and I urge showing up on other professed churchgoers who don't show up nearly as often as they think or say they do. I'll get into a bit of why I believe in showing up in the next chapter.

Yet I wonder, what are we really expecting to accomplish with our outbound communication?

Is "show up" the best first message to send to that anonymous person who just "met" our church online, especially given the intensifying societal pull away from showing up?

What do we expect to happen as a result of the person showing up if they go against the tide and actually do show up?

What foundation are we laying in the life of a disciple-in-the-making when the primary instruction we give them (and never stop giving them) is to show up?

Finally, is "show up" the message that Jesus commissioned his apostles—and all of us, his followers—to proclaim?

2

OUR "WHY" PROBLEM

The Suspect Sacrament of Showing Up

In the previous chapter I argued that the vast bulk of outbound church communication is to get people to show up. I actually didn't argue this point very far because I believe that the phenomenon is self-evident to anyone accustomed to working in a church.

I also claimed that we who work in the church are increasingly failing to get people to show up due to huge, complex societal forces that resist our efforts. We don't have to fully name and explain them to feel them when we press up against them.

But there are other reasons that the "show up" strategy is increasingly ineffective. These reasons don't have to do with the sea-change shifts of our era; rather, they have to do with dissonance between our approach and the mission of Jesus that he founded his church to continue for the last 2,000 years. In short, our communication is not as effective as we'd like it to be because we aren't doing it his way.

Now, in what follows I don't want to be misunderstood. Please do not hear me saying that the "show up" communications approach *never* works or *never has* worked in any period of Christian history. That is patently false.

Nor am I saying that there is *no* place for communications that try to get people to show up. Of course there is! Churches do put on events—some on a weekly rhythm, some occasional events and one-offs—and they have to let people know that they're happening. This is an essential component of the overall communications mix.

What I *am* saying, however, is that our default communications approach rests on a set of unexamined and untenable assumptions. I am saying that when the "show up" approach has worked in the past—I mean *truly* worked according to kingdom-of-God standards—it has ridden on top of a whole lot of less obvious activity that we can't assume it is resting on in our place and day. And I am saying that the current sociocultural shift that inhibits people from showing up isn't creating a weakness in how we do church so much as *exposing a weakness that was already there.*

A communication strategy built on "show up"—whether explicit or, more often, implicit and assumed—has three problems:

- **A problem with our *why*.** Getting people to show up doesn't accomplish as much as we hope it will.

- **A problem with our *how*.** We are trying to get people to show up to a program, but we are expecting too much of our programs.

- **A problem with our *what*.** When our communication revolves around showing up, we unavoidably promote the wrong thing.

This chapter is about our *why* problem. Quite simply, our hope is misplaced. We expect a lot more to happen when people show up than we can reasonably expect it to deliver.

The Sacrament of Showing Up

A rough-and-ready definition of *sacrament* in Christian theology is that it is a standardized, ritual procedure through which, when humans perform it, God supernaturally does something that changes people spiritually beyond what we can see with our natural eyes (at least so long as the properly authorized people do it the right way).

Catholics' understanding of salvation is deeply intertwined with a thoroughly elaborated sacramental system. Protestants have been skeptical of that system. Some are comfortable with the concept of sacrament but keep it within narrower limits both in the number of sacraments and in what a sacrament is expected to accomplish. Others, especially in the United States, narrow their eyes at the mere mention of the word "sacrament" and completely reject the notion.

Or do they?

I had an evangelism professor in seminary who was friends with a Catholic priest. One day the priest told the professor, "You evangelicals are always busting our chops for our seven sacraments. Well at least we have *seven*. You have only one!" The professor had no idea what he was talking about. "'Pray this prayer after me,'" the priest continued. "*One* sacrament."

We could add to that "sacrament" "come to the 'altar' during this song" or "with every head bowed and every eye closed, put up your hand" or "throw a pinecone into the campfire" or "check a box on the response card." As it turns out, it's hard to live without sacraments since we can't peer directly into the human spirit. We so yearn to see some tangible evidence that God is at work that we are prone to identify a ritual act (though we would never call it that) as proof positive that a person has experienced the new birth, now and forever.

Likewise, we so yearn to see God work that we are prone to construct a set of procedures that generate new births when properly followed. At the heart of many of these is the sacrament of showing up. The idea is that, if a person shows up to our event, spiritual rebirth and growth are likely to happen. If a person shows up to the event a lot of times, then there's an even greater likelihood that it will happen. And if a person shows up to a great variety of our events with regularity, then it's virtually assured that it has happened.

When Showing Up Worked

This notion isn't entirely crazy, though it does trace back to a rather crazy time in the history of American Christianity—I actually mean "crazy" in a good way.

For the first hundred years of the evangelical movement in the English-speaking world (roughly 1730–1830), believers were fascinated—sometimes obsessed—with the opaque barrier between the spiritual condition of the inner person and outward behavior that could be observed and manipulated. For example, they wondered what the signs were that a person was saved; they especially wondered what the signs were that *they themselves* were saved. They also wondered at how God sometimes brought spiritual awakening on a whole church or town or nation at his own pleasure, seemingly out of nowhere, which humans could not engineer or predict.

That mindset of marveling at the mystery of God's transforming work changed in the nineteenth century, and the main person associated with the change is Charles Grandison Finney (1792–1875). Finney famously and scandalously claimed that a revival was not a miracle. Yet it's important to observe what he meant by that. He did *not* mean that God didn't make revival happen. Rather, he meant that God makes a revival happen just as God makes a plant grow. If a farmer fertilizes soil and tills it and plants a seed and waters it and nurtures it, it's going to grow. The farmer doesn't make the plant grow; he only follows the procedures God designed. Yet if he does, the plant will assuredly grow. In the same way, Finney claimed, if Christians simply follow the procedures God designed, God will assuredly send revival.[3]

According to Finney, one of those divinely designed procedures was united, believing, corporate prayer—a lot of it. (Finney found women to be especially good at getting together to do this.) But another procedure was a "protracted meeting" of worship services on four consecutive days. Yet another was an "anxious bench" at the service where people who were worried about the state of their souls would sit until they felt something change within.

Our sacramental procedures have changed since Finney's day (and not altogether for the better—it is exceedingly rare to find people who pray as Finney and his colleagues did). But you can see how we are living out the echo of the Second Great Awakening when Finney's approach was a smashing success. We still heavily operate by an event-centered ministry model. We still are convinced that if we can just get someone to the event and run the event the right way, good things are likely to happen.

And by the way, this is not a knock on the so-called "attractional church" exclusively. There are churches that don't draw people the same way and don't shape worship the same way as "attractional" churches do that nevertheless operate according to the very same hope. Meanwhile, churches that attempt to be "missional" in contradistinction to "attractional" ones frequently slip into the same event-based groove, especially when the application of "mission" remains rather superficial. Whether *we go to the people* in a missional event in the community or *they come to us* for an attractional event on church grounds, we're still hoping that people will "show up" and that great things will happen as a result.

A Much Bigger Kind of Showing Up

Once again, let me be clear: sometimes God *does* do awesome things when people show up! Sometimes people *are* converted that way. People who show up often over a long period of time, especially to a mix of worship services, small groups, and service opportunities, *are* likely to be influenced for the better as a result.

However, when God does great things through "showing up," it generally is not because showing up is sacramental. It's generally because other stuff is going on before, during, and after the event. We may pay lip-service to that stuff, but we often don't concentrate our time, energy, effort, resources, and hope on it, because we are consumed by the demands of the event. "Showing up" might bring just enough energy for spiritual ignition in a person's life, but when it works, the fuel was already painstakingly gathered, prepared, and arranged and was probably even beginning to smoke when the event took place.

Along these lines, let's return to that famous Woody Allen quote—"Showing up is 80 percent of life"—for a closer look.

Allen was speaking tersely and casually when he coined this phrase, so out of context it conveys very little of what he originally meant. At the time, Allen was talking about the advice he gave young playwrights. "My observation," Allen clarified later, "was that once a person actually completed a play or a novel he was well on his way to getting it produced or published, as opposed to a vast majority of people who tell me their ambition is to write, but who strike out on the very first level and indeed never write the play or book."[4]

So what kind of "showing up" was Allen talking about? He didn't mean that 80 percent of life was merely being present, and then good stuff happens. He meant showing up *with a completed script or novel!* "Showing up" to Woody Allen referred to the long, arduous, toilsome process of fashioning a complete product. *That is 80 percent of succeeding in life.*

Similarly, when God does something supernatural in a person who shows up to one of our events, it is the result of a long process of craftsmanship—not principally the crafting of our event but the crafting *of the person.* That craftsmanship may take place before we encounter the person—in fact, it *always* does to a great degree—but a disciple-making ministry that works over the long haul generally involves God using *us* to do a significant portion of the crafting.

Showing Up to Jesus

Before we move on from the "sacrament of showing up," here's one more point to consider. If showing up yields such fine results, then the person who should have seen the best results was Jesus. If there really is any such thing as a sacrament—divine, transforming power conveyed through tangible, physical means—the Incarnate Word himself is the supreme sacrament. So "showing up" to him should be supremely effective.

But Jesus had thousands of people "show up" to him, and only a few hundred were true disciples at the end. And not once in the Gospels did he instruct his apostles, "As the Father sent me, I am sending you into all the earth . . . to get people to show up. Whatever you do, guys, make sure you do that."

The presupposition that showing up makes a person into a disciple is backwards. Rather, being a disciple makes a person show up.

So if our communication revolves around "showing up," our *why* is wrong. Because even if our communication succeeds in getting people to show up . . . well, where does that get us?

3

OUR "HOW" PROBLEM

Why Discipleship Programs Don't Make Disciples

In the last chapter, I claimed that a communication strategy built on "show up" has a problem with our *why*, our *how*, and our *what*. I then detailed our "why" problem: our reason for getting people to show up is off the mark, because we think showing up accomplishes more than it actually does.

In this chapter I want to explore the next problem with the "show up" strategy: our "how"—or, our method. Just as we make a great effort to get people to show up, we also make a great effort to give them something to show up *to*: a program. We hope the program will take them the rest of the way. Yet our hope is misplaced.

The Result Matches the Method   *Awana?*

What I mean by a "program" is an activity organized by church leaders for people in the church or recruited by the church, usually for a scheduled time and place. Optimally, the activity is something that disciples of Jesus do because they are (or are becoming) disciples of Jesus.

"Show up"-centered communication is one link in a strategic

chain that typically looks something like this:

Communication ("Show Up!")

Program 0 (Outreach Event—Optional)

Program 1 (Worship)

**Program 2 (Small Group or Volunteer Service
or Membership Class)**

Program 3 (Another One of the Above)

Program 4 (the Last of the Above)

**Program 5 (Retreat and/or Conference and/or
Short-Term Missions Trip—Optional)**

**Result: A Soul-Winning, Disciple-Making,
Missional, Relational-Evangelism Dynamo**

What do you notice about this strategy? The thing that stands out to me the most is the dissonance between the method and the intended outcome. We're using a particular process to make a disciple, but we're expecting that person to make disciples by a different process than the one that made him or her.

Our method is:

- corporate

- orderly

- initiated by an authority figure/purveyor

- group-sized

- scheduled

- located in places that a person needs to get themselves to

Yet we hope to produce a disciple who makes disciples by a different method, a method that is:

- personal

- non-linear

- self-directed

- one-on-one

- spontaneous (in many or most situations)

- located where people already are (that is, until the person can pop the question, "Want to come to church?")

Why do we expect our method to yield our intended result? As W. E. Deming pithily said, "Your system is perfectly designed to give you the results you're getting."

Stages of Spiritual Maturity

To be fair, it's not as though this method yields *nothing* that we want. Of course some converts and mature Jesus-followers have emerged out of the tail end of this pipeline. So it takes closer investigation to figure out why the mature believers manufactured by the model tend not to be prolific disciple-makers.

The last ten years or so in the ministry world have witnessed a steep increase of interest in discipleship. A number of the authors who have multiplied books on the subject attempt to schematize the progression of a disciple in generic, recognizable stages. There are many commonalities among these various schemas. The one I believe to be most helpful—especially for my purposes here—is by Bobby Harrington and Greg Wiens in their e-book *Becoming a Disciple Maker*.[5]

Harrington and Wiens delineate a generic, six-stage (or "-level") sequence of spiritual maturation using the analogy of physical maturation:

- **Level 0 – Spiritually Dead** (or "spiritually unborn"). This person is still "dead in their transgressions and sins" (Eph. 2:1) and has not yet been born from above by the Spirit.

- **Level 1 – Spiritual Infant.** This person has experienced the new birth and is full of excitement about the Lord, but they usually have plenty of unsound, culturally conditioned beliefs and ungodly lifestyle habits.

- **Level 2 – Spiritual Child.** This person has a sound hold on the rudiments Christian teaching, conforms reasonably well in behavior, and is solidly connected to a body of believers. However, the person is basically engaged in Christianity for what they get out of it, even when they volunteer. They are likely to agree that Christianity is "an important part of my life," which means that it competes with other priorities of similar or greater importance.

- **Level 3 – Spiritual Young Adult.** This person has moved from "Christianity is an important part of my life" to "Christ is my life." They give sacrificially of time, talent, and treasure for the kingdom and serve the church diligently, but despite endeavoring to bear witness to Christ, they have little experience leading anyone along his way.

- **Level 4 – Spiritual Parent.** While (or despite) continuing to serve in the machinery of church, this person's main, focused contribution to the kingdom is in the individuals they are winning to Christ and teaching to obey everything he commands.

- **Level 5 – Spiritual Grandparent.** This person has been making disciples with enough perseverance over enough time to have successfully taught their disciples to make disciples.

I present this schema because it provides the categories for understanding why the typical programmatic method does not produce disciple-makers. In brief, we are hoping for Level-4 and Level-5 believers from a ministry model that at best maxes out at Level 3.

Why People Stop at Level 3

Imagine a person who works their way through part or even all of the programmatic process of the church because they respond well to the summons to show up. Most likely, along the way they will likely have some amount of meaningful personal interaction with disciples of Jesus. For example, a person might invite them to an event or even to life in Christ. Or they might find a teacher they become particularly attached to. Nevertheless, let's assume that the weight of emphasis is on participation in the programs themselves.

First, we have to acknowledge that many people who are trained from the beginning that their number-one job is to show up will not do more than show up. That's all they will ever do; they're not going to proceed past Level 1. More than that is not what they signed up for and not what they thought they were being offered. They may even cite your own biblical preaching to validate that they don't need to do anything more to "earn their way into heaven." So why should they?

Some people in the program pipeline proceed to Level 2, but in essence that level of maturity merely involves showing up to more things more often. They get a greater benefit from the programs than they did before, and they may have their mind and behavior significantly reshaped. However, their reason for sticking around largely hangs on whether the church programs they're showing up to are superior to the other, non-church things they might show up to—and also superior to staying home.

Nevertheless, the church's programs do produce some Level-3 Christians, especially among those who have cultivated personal relationships as they've moved through the programs. In other words, what keeps them around isn't just the programs or a particular preaching personality; it's also the people. These programs and people are important instruments that God used to shift them into a Christ-centered life.

The people at Level 3 are the sort of people that every pastor wants. They are the hard workers, the leaders, the pillars. But what is it that they're working for, leading, and upholding?

You guessed it: the programs.

Good students are loyal to good teachers and want to be like them; good children are loyal to good parents and want to be like them. So if a person is grown in the faith by a set of programs, they're going to devote themselves loyally to maintaining the programs that raised them.

Now that's good as far as it goes . . . but that's about as far as it goes. Spiritual young adults have spiritual maturity, wisdom, and power. What they don't have is spiritual children.

Actually, that's not quite true. Level-3 disciples tend to raise their biological children as their spiritual children. Unlike people at Level 1 who have no spiritual impact on their children and those at Level 2 who tend to raise nominal Christians, Level-3 believers disciple their young—with the help of church programs, of course. The biological offspring of spiritual young adults make up the bulk of the servants of the church in the next generation.

A continuous flow of biological children of Level-3 disciples has historically sustained churches—at least as long as both the birth rate and respect from the wider culture stay up. Unfortunately, today both have dropped considerably. Moreover, even at the best of times believers at Level 3 alone have never driven a disciple-making movement of the gospel. Without disciples at Levels 4 and 5, it doesn't happen.

It's not that Christians at Level 3 don't know that they ought to be making disciples of unbelievers outside their nuclear families. They know it acutely, agree with it wholeheartedly, and are shamed by it continually. It's not as though they don't try to do it either. Unfortunately, their number-one obstacle to moving to Level 4— spiritual parenthood—is that they weren't raised to spiritual maturity by a spiritual parent in the first place. They were raised by a program, so they replicate what they know. Like sterile worker bees, they build the hive and supply the pollen, but they don't expand the colony.

The saddest thing that can happen to a spiritual young adult, especially as they age, is that they sometimes become highly attached to programs (and their institutional habitat) in lieu of the mission that the programs are intended to advance. Their spiritual nursery becomes a prison, but they don't see it that way. They see it as home, and woe to the leader who attempts to change it.

Another Way to Make Disciples

To sum up the foregoing, people make disciples who make disciples, but programs make disciples who make programs.

There *is* another way, however. That way is *not* to abandon programs. It is rather for programs to assume their proper place. It isn't a question of programs *or* disciple-making. It is a question of emphasis. Where personal, relational disciple-making is primary, programs are very valuable vehicles for it. They serve as wonderful environments for making disciples, and the formal content supplied in them makes for wonderful tools.

But as long as programs are primary, the main communication message is to show up. And as long as the communications message is to show up, programs will remain primary.

When personal disciple-making lives, programs will live. Yet when programs live, disciple-making may die. Or as Mike Breen says—perhaps overstating it but with justification—"If you make disciples, you always get the church. But if you make a church, you rarely get disciples."

4

OUR "WHAT" PROBLEM

The Captivating Alternative to Proclaiming Ourselves

"We do not proclaim ourselves," Paul wrote, "but Jesus Christ as Lord" (2 Cor. 4:5).

I've pondered this verse a good deal as I've thought about church communication. Treating my ministry neighbor as I'd like to be treated and giving them the benefit of the doubt, I like to think that the main message in most church buildings on most Sundays is that Jesus Christ is Lord.

But I don't see this message *outside* most buildings. On advertising platforms from websites to billboards, I see churches proclaiming themselves. On their changeable-letter roadside signs, I see churches proclaiming themselves—unless they've opted instead to make criminally corny puns.

By "proclaiming themselves" I mean projecting the continual message to show up: "We're doing something good! You want to be here (at thus-and-such a time)!" Yet this message composes the third problem with a communication strategy centered on "show up"—the *what* problem. "Show up" is the substitute for proclaiming Christ as Lord.

25

If I Sound Overly Harsh . . .

There are two legitimate objections to the charge I've alleged, and I want to honor both.

One objection may be raised by a small minority of churches that have begun experimenting with a testimonial-based marketing approach. Some churches are doing more with their website than simply announcing what a great church they are and what events people ought to show up to. These churches present stories from real, highly relatable participants in their churches about why those people like the church so much.

I want to say on record that I think that this technique is excellent, and I wish more churches would use it. It's a very winsome, compelling, and human way to present the message, and I love how it helps the reader or viewer picture themselves in the church. It lowers inhibitions and barriers and raises comfort, and this is all to the good.

Nevertheless, in the end, it's just a more powerful way of proclaiming ourselves. It's still *we* telling *them* how awesome we are. Once again, as I said in chapter 1, this isn't altogether bad. Talking about ourselves and encouraging people to show up is an important part of church communication. The problem is when it is the dominant part or even the only part.

The other objection could be voiced by a much broader sweep of churches—possibly all of them. That objection is that we aren't proclaiming ourselves because we're so in love with ourselves and think we're the greatest. Rather, we're proclaiming ourselves to draw a crowd so that we can proclaim Jesus to them. We proclaim ourselves in a big way outside—with a little bit of Jesus on our "About Us" webpages with doctrine, mission and values, and so forth—so that we can proclaim Jesus in a big way inside.

Naturally, this is the ministry model that undergirds "show up" communication: get them here so that good things will happen. But I'd like to suggest that drawing a crowd is one problem we do *not* have. That's one area where we've already succeeded.

Who Is the Crowd?

You might be incredulous at my claim. After all, didn't I speak in an earlier chapter about how people are leaving their homes less to do *anything*, much less come to church? And aren't we seeing smaller crowds in our worship settings every year?

It's hard not to be envious of Jesus on this point, isn't it? Now there was a guy who had no trouble drawing a crowd. I mean, when you're the only really effective health care dispensary in the world—and you are really, *really* effective—you're going to have a crowd around you all the time.

The example of Jesus drives some—I think it should drive all of us—to seek the power of the Holy Spirit to make people miraculously whole in our place and day. Yet while miracles and healings may have considerable value to authenticate our message to those open to believing it, we don't need miracles to draw a crowd any more than we need a huge marketing budget.

See, it all comes down to what we mean by a "crowd."

In the Gospels, when Jesus is followed by a "crowd" or "crowds" (also known as a "multitude" or "multitudes"), it certainly means a large number of people. But that's not all the crowd was. "The crowd" could also mean the mass of people outside the inner circle. It meant the common people as opposed to the ruling authorities. Since in Judea the ruling authorities under Roman supervision were the families from which chief priests were chosen (Sadducees) plus the strict-living scholars of Torah (Pharisees), to that elite "the crowd" meant the vast bulk of Jews who were less holy and less learned than they were.[6]

To Jesus also, "the crowd" consisted of the mass of outsiders who were less holy and less learned than the insiders. The big difference is that Jesus revolutionized what the center of the circle was—namely, himself—and who was qualified to enter it.

We'll get to that in a bit. The important thing for the moment, however, is that from this angle, "the crowd" is not about *quantity of people* but about *quality of people*. If you are with one solitary person who is outside the kingdom of God and does not understand its mysteries—as Jesus was with the woman at the well in John 4—then you are with "the crowd."

When you look at it this way, it becomes obvious that each of us has already drawn a crowd. Each of us has "crowd" people—Level-0 people—among those who come and go through our physical and social media presence. Granted, some believers are so entwined in a relational web of Christians that they have very few of the crowd within arm's length. But even for those believers, "crowd people" are usually still visible if they try to see them and count them.

The crowd is there. We don't have to go get them. We're already living among them. They are already drawn to us, whether by compulsion, happenstance, or attraction.

This idea has the potential to turn church communication inside out. The institutional hub's emphasis shifts from proclaiming itself to draw a crowd to supplying church members with the words to proclaim Christ to the microcrowds they've already gathered. Then church members' proclamation out among the crowd leaves a trail of bread crumbs to the mass proclamatory event on Sunday morning.

Jesus' Message to the Crowd

So let's say that each of us is supposed to proclaim Jesus Christ as Lord to our own personal crowd. What did Jesus himself proclaim to the crowd? According to his model, what is it that the crowd needs to hear?

It might surprise you that even though Jesus spent countless hours talking to the crowd, we actually know little of what he said that was directed mainly to them. If we look carefully at the clues in the Gospels and piece them together, we find that the content of the Gospels is heavily back-loaded with the period of Jesus' ministry *after* he called disciples—especially the Twelve—who listened very carefully to remember everything he was saying. A swift reading of the Gospels makes it look as if that late period started five minutes after Jesus' baptism, but a closer study reveals that his eventual disciples didn't go from hanging around him to leaving their jobs for him for a long time after Jesus began teaching—maybe even as long as two years.[7]

It also happens that during this same, latter period, Jesus spoke to the crowd (outsiders) less and to his disciples (insiders) more. Even the famed Sermon on the Mount, though it was heard by the crowd, was actually *overheard*, as it was a message Jesus delivered to his disciples with the crowd listening in.[8]

Nevertheless, despite the relative scarcity of examples, we do know the basics of the message he delivered to the crowd. Aside from statements he made to individual sick and bereaved people in the crowd (for example, "Stand up, take your stretcher, and walk"—Mark 2:9), Jesus communicated three things that he believed were crucial for the crowd to know.

First, Jesus talked about **the imminent arrival of the kingdom of God** (in all the Gospels but especially in Matthew, Mark, and Luke). He and his audience shared a belief from the prophets that the awesome day of the Lord would usher in a new order that would solve all the problems of the people who were faithfully devoted to God. Jesus asserted that this new order, the kingdom, had almost arrived. He also used provocative analogies to expand minds and shake up misconceptions about what it would be like.

The call to action from his teaching about the kingdom was to *repent.* That meant that a person changed their mind and their ways to conform to the new reality so that they would have a stake in it and not be excluded from it.

Second, Jesus talked about *himself* (in all the Gospels but especially in John). He portrayed himself as the unique figure who brought the kingdom to the people (by his incarnation and later his second coming) and who brought people into the kingdom (by his death, resurrection, and ascension). People naturally drew the conclusion that Jesus was the Messiah ("Christ") though he was different in many ways from what they had expected the Messiah would be. Jesus said little to affirm their conclusion straight on, but he deliberately said and did all sorts of provocative things that encouraged it.

The call to action from Jesus' teaching about himself was to *believe*. That meant believing his unique role in history, his unique relationship with God his Father, and his unique authority over all things. Above all, it meant believing that Jesus is the unique way a person can come to inherit eternal life in the kingdom.

Third, Jesus talked about *right behavior*. What we often miss looking in on the world of the Gospels from the outside is that this was a very hot topic in Jesus' day. Most Jews believed in a coming kingdom. Many believed that the behavior of the Jewish people influenced or even determined how long it would take for God to send it. Most also believed that their faithfulness to God's Law would make or break whether Jews even continued to exist as a people amid the pervasive influence of Greek culture.

So questions of right behavior according to Torah,[9] even small questions, had huge consequences. They were also highly practical questions that touched every part of life—down to, "How often am I supposed to wash this pot?" Many people really cared about questions about the Law. They weren't academic: they were among the "felt needs" of Jesus' place and day.

Jesus' answers to people's questions about the right ("lawful") way to live were highly original. It's not that he had no similarities to other teachers. It's that the peculiar combination of overarching principles that Jesus applied to Torah was a one-of-a-kind set. For example, Jesus' ethical teaching had more in common with the

Pharisees' than with anyone, yet in other respects he was so different from the Pharisees that they were enraged at him more than anyone else was.

Jesus' principles for interpreting Torah make for a very interesting topic, but it belongs in another book. What ought to be seen here, however, is that Jesus' teaching about right behavior lined up with *his teaching about the kingdom.* His ethics rested on the reality of the kingdom and formed the concrete action steps of his call to *repent.*

Yet Jesus' teaching about Torah also lined up with *his teaching about himself,* because he presented himself as having unique and supreme authority to interpret Torah. A person would only live out Torah Jesus' way if the person *believed* that Jesus was who he said he was.

A kin to us teaching "Jesus Transforms."

Our Common Ground with the Crowd

So how do we take what Jesus proclaimed to the crowd of his place and day and apply it to what we are to proclaim to the crowd around us?

The first thing we must recognize is that Jesus spoke to the crowd according to the common ground he shared with the crowd: (1) belief in a coming kingdom and (2) the Scriptures (what we call the Old Testament) as the critical guide for living. This common ground wasn't trite or ho-hum; it was on everybody's mind as the pressing issues of the day.

The next thing we must recognize is that the common ground that Jesus had with his crowd is not the same as the common ground we have with ours. The people in the crowd around us aren't eagerly waiting for the prophesied, kingly government of God to break in and replace our governments, and they don't believe that the Bible is the critical guide for right behavior. So we might conclude that we need a different message for our crowd than Jesus delivered to his.

Or do we?

It's true that people in our crowd are not yearning for the prophetic hope of the day of the Lord. But there remains a strong hope for *a better future*, generally speaking.

True, at the big level—globally, nationally—fewer people believe in a better future than they used to. We live in a cynical age that feels far removed from the utopias hoped in by 20th-century people. But many, many people still believe—or want to believe— in a better future for their own life or their family's life. They might not believe in a better future on the big scale, but they do hope for it on the small scale. I think that even embittered people who *don't* believe in a better future are bitter mainly because they believe it *should* exist, or that it exists for some people but not others, and they feel cheated or excluded.

Similarly, it is true that people in our crowd don't believe that the Bible is the authoritative guide for right living—and when they do, "the Bible" is usually just an unfamiliar abstraction. Most (not all) don't have more than a childish grasp of it, they don't read it, they cherry-pick what they want out of it, and they don't put much effort into improving how they practice it in scope, scale, and consistency.

Yet all sorts of people are acutely concerned about the right way to live. They tend not to think about that in terms of ethics and morals. (Though they do believe in morals: they're the principles that they follow and that the bad guys—however defined—don't.) For the present-day crowd, "the right way to live" generally isn't the *moral* way to live under the watchful eye of a divine Judge. Rather, it is the *successful* way to live. In other words, the "right way to live" consists of the set of techniques that carries oneself to the better future.

From "Show Up" to "Try This"

I believe that this is all the common ground we need with the crowds that have been drawn around each us. We, like the crowd, are looking for the better future, even if we trace it on a vastly bigger canvas. And we, like the crowd, want to know and follow the right way to live, even if we believe that that way covers much more territory and that the stakes of following it or not are far higher.

In addition to the necessary messages to show up, church communication to the crowd that is faithful and effective in the 21st century must feature counsel on the right techniques of life to arrive at a better future. In short, *we must shift from "show up" to "grow up"*—and "grow up" really means *"try this."*

However, just as Jesus did, we must sketch techniques for living that startle and upend what is normal—that describe an alternative way to live that both works in this reality and is bracingly alien to it. We must also suggest a better future that is bigger, deeper, and wilder than most people are bold enough to hope for.

And just as Jesus did, we must give tantalizing hints—without coming out and saying it bluntly at first—that Jesus is the one who makes the better future a reality. We must lead people who wish to "taste and see"—people who try out Jesus' principles in their lives before they've decisively repented and believed him—to the place where the Lord of glory is revealed to their eyes.

In sum, 21st-century church communication must give church members something to talk about outside the church with their microcrowds. That conversation establishes the credibility of both the gospel and the church before a "crowd person" directly encounters either. It eventually sets up a personal invitation to Christ or to the gatherings where Christ is boldly proclaimed.

Part 2 is about how to equip believers for that conversation.

Part 2

The Church's Content Solution

5

WHERE DID ALL THE TRACTS GO?

How to Make an Evangelistic Toolbox for 21st-Century People

When was the last time you used an evangelistic tract to share the gospel with someone?

I'd better stop before I begin, because depending on your age, you might not know what I'm talking about. So let me start over.

(Deep breath.)

Back in the 20th century there were these tiny booklets called "tracts." A tract was very short—usually between six and ten pages long—and when closed it was about the size of a 3-by-5 index card. It fit in your breast pocket.

A tract outlined the gospel so that an unbeliever would understand it and commit their life to Christ. Some tracts were something like a narrative essay embedded in a real-life story or some relatable analogy—sort of like a mini-sermon in print. These were best deployed by leaving them on a table in the doctor's office or on a seat on the bus or on the commode in a public restroom so that the next person might pick it up and read it.

Other tracts—most notably, the famed *Four Spiritual Laws*—were more like miniature PowerPoint presentations. They had a series of Scripture-studded diagrams on facing pages so that with every flip of the page you got the next "slide," the next important point of the gospel. These were best used as visual aids in a direct one-to-one encounter.

The tract was the universal evangelistic tool of the mid- to late 20th century. If you're middle-aged or older today, and you've been in the church for a long time, you can remember a time when evangelism was virtually defined as approaching someone (including a total stranger—fun!), running them through a gospel tract, and popping the question, "Do you want to receive Christ as your personal Lord and Savior?" If you were an especially obedient or zealous Christian, you did this at least once.

And that may have worked, because it did from time to time. A lot of people were saved this way—or at least so we were told. Or if you were like me (and I think most people were) you didn't have that kind of success yourself. But you heard lots of encouraging stories about how some person heard the gospel because someone shared a tract with them; they rejected it at first but the message kept gnawing at them; and then the next person who shared the gospel with them hit paydirt and the person believed. You may have hoped that you were a link in that kind of chain. I did—and who knows, maybe we were!

It's also possible that you had a moment of success when someone prayed to receive Christ at the end of the tract. But then they didn't do what they were supposed to do: they didn't go to church with you or read their Bible or get together to learn how to grow in their faith, and you didn't have categories to make sense of what went wrong.

Tracts weren't perfect tools, but they were powerful tools for a significant period of time. And then, almost overnight, many people stopped using them and stopped urging and training others to do the same. Our model of evangelism was so tied to the tract that when the tract went away it almost seemed as if evangelism itself went away.

Why Don't We Use Tracts Anymore?

Maybe evangelism *did* go away. There's an argument to be made that the main reason few of us use tracts anymore is that few of us evangelize anymore. Then again, it's possible that few of us evangelized much after the Jesus Movement went quiet, and what looked like evangelism in the 1980s and '90s was only a few tract-brandishers who tried in vain to mobilize the rest of us.

Nevertheless, there was another popular evangelistic technique in those days: the mass evangelistic preaching event. In that technique, the job of the rank-and-file was to invite people (yet again) to "show up." By the end of the century, the mass evangelistic event had become rather sneaky. ("Show up to our 'family festival'! There will be face-painting for the kids!" Then—wham!—hit the captive audience with the gospel.) By that time, however, the seeker-sensitive movement had started taking off, so many believers shifted from inviting people to evangelistic events to inviting people to their rapidly growing, felt-needsy, "relevant," adult-contemporary weekend church service.

Meanwhile, the tract languished from disuse, and not just because people had a ready alternative (specifically, "Please just show up; my teaching pastor will do the hard part"). The real reason we stopped using tracts was that they weren't effective anymore. In some ways the tract was ideal for its time, but times changed. In other ways it was flawed from the start, and the changing times revealed the flaws.

So why don't most of us use tracts today?

1. **It moves too fast.** Think of what a tract attempts to accomplish in sales terms. A tract tries to establish rapport, address a felt need, identify a deeper need,

present the solution to that need, and win the biggest commitment a person will ever make in their life, all in six pages. That is the shortest sales funnel in history.

2. **Its message is simplistic.** The tract grew up in the era when the "simple gospel" was popular. I'm referring to the democratic wisdom of trusting the common folk and being skeptical of the intelligentsia, of lauding the gospel for being "so simple a child can understand it" and rejecting anything complex or paradoxical. This impulse has some legitimacy, and without a doubt simplicity is powerful and necessary to communicate a new idea effectively. But it ignores the extraordinary depth and nuance of the gospel and is completely unequipped to address the questions and doubts of someone operating from a completely different base of assumptions. Once, that sort of person was the exception in the culturally Christian crowd; now that person is the norm.

3. **It isn't relational.** More precisely, the tract didn't *have to be* relational. The tract was sometimes very effective as a tool applied at just the right moment in a full-orbed, evolving friendship. But the tract was often deployed with (or maybe *against*) fragile new relationships and even total strangers. In other words, you were trying to have a conversation about the most sensitive area of a person's life when you barely knew the person's name. That was a tough sell in the best of times, but today, with people being much keener about personal authenticity than about propositional truth, it's a door-slammer.

4. **Its delivery is awkward.** Sure, you can leave a tract in a public place, and maybe someone will pick it up. But if you want someone you know to read it, you have to hold it open and say, "Want to look at this with me?" That's a

rather uncommon and clumsy social gesture today.

5. **Its technology is passé.** In the 19th century, mass-produced leaflets and pamphlets were the cutting edge of communications technology. In the 20th century it was a stale but still common way to get a message out. Not anymore.

6. **It's church-optional.** Yes, it was possible to stamp your church's name and address on the back of a tract, but it looked rather out of place. Tracts grew up in the era when the profile of parachurch eclipsed church in American evangelical life. Parachurch organizations did the most to develop the tract; they printed and branded them; and they used them most effectively. There was little natural, visual draw from a tract to a church body, and many who prayed the prayer at the end didn't wind up in one.

The Advantages of the Written Word

Nevertheless, despite all the problems with tracts that keep us from using them, the concept itself is a good one. For a multitude of ordinary Christians, it is truly helpful to have some piece of content to bridge the gap between their friendship with an unbeliever and a conversation about Christ and the difference he makes. For most people, going at evangelism without a tool is like going into a fast-paced hockey game without pads and skates. They're not going in at all—it's too dangerous! Or at best they go in with the "show up" approach.

So the question remains, what would a 21st-century "neotract" look like? What tool can serve the same function without the old version's flaws?

Video is a hot ticket right now, and some highly creative people are doing some outstanding work with animated videos distributed online. (Although their work is aimed more at insiders than at outsiders, The Bible Project is a sterling example.) Similarly, podcasts are getting bigger all the time as the accompaniment for the driving and exercising that people are doing as much as ever. And infographics can make very powerful and memorable messages, although they tend more toward displaying quantifiable data.

Nevertheless, the technology of the written word isn't outmoded just yet. Written content has two peculiar advantages that have not yet been superseded by other media.

First, for the literate, writing is the best medium for the shortest attention span and time investment. That's because written text is supremely skimmable, especially when it is formatted in a way that draws attention to the key points. A person might look at a four-minute video and say, "I don't have time." But the same person might open a blog post because they can scan headers and bulleted lists in 30 seconds to decide whether it's worth reading more carefully.

Second, writing can be referred to again quickly. Text is eminently searchable—you don't need to have the title memorized—and it is easy to locate exactly the part you wanted another look at. By contrast, have you ever tried to find the part in that one video or podcast episode where the person says that one thing . . . ? Most of us don't recall that it came at 11 minutes, 37 seconds.

Anatomy of a Neotract

The technology of literacy remains relevant, and written content retains value. So what are the characteristics of writing that will communicate to the 21st-century "crowd" as Jesus would?

The "neotract" that I envision looks like this:

- an approximately 1,000-word blog post, well-formatted for skimming

Cool

- a topic drawn from "felt needs"—that is, ordinary, modern people's hope for a better personal future

- a gripping, technique-oriented headline

- located on a church's website with its identity clearly emblazoned on the page header

- shared on social media by committed church leaders, members, and even newcomers for the "crowds" they're connected to

The goal is to provide content that is eminently clickable and genuinely valuable to all sorts of people. This can tee up spiritual conversations between readers and their Christian friends when the unbeliever comments on the post on the believer's social media feed or when the believer shares it directly with the person. ("Hey, I read this today and I thought of you, from when we were talking about . . . .") When a disciple and a not-yet-disciple dialogue over how the substance of the post applies to their lives, it becomes a ready-made opportunity for the believer to share their hope in Christ freely and naturally.

In addition, when people enjoy a sequence of neotracts repeatedly over time, they are likely to gain increasingly positive feelings toward the church that is posting them. That growing positive association may produce a much greater inclination to respond positively when the reader is invited to "show up" at the preaching event. They might respond, "The stuff your church posts makes sense. If your pastor talks about stuff like that, I'll give it a try."

Getting the technical details of delivery nailed down is relatively easy. The tricky part is the content itself. It's not easy to provide a down-to-earth question with a down-to-earth answer that is genuinely shaped by the gospel but isn't explicit and confrontational. (The explicit part comes later, in a personal relationship.) So in the next chapter we'll look at the principles of how it's done.

6

JESUS IS THE ANSWERS

How the Gospel Provides Multiple Solutions to Everyday Problems

A glass case in the Paterson Museum in Paterson, New Jersey contains a healthy number of boring-looking, nondescript rocks. Why these rocks would sit on display in a museum is totally obscure until the docent turns out the lights and turns on an ultraviolet lamp above the case. Immediately, deep red, lime green, and electric purple flourescent minerals embedded in the rocks burn spectacularly through the darkness.

These rocks come from New Jersey's Franklin and Sterling Hill mines, which contain the largest number of mineral species found in one place in the world, including dozens that have never been discovered anywhere else. The rare and mesmerizing beauty of the ore from these mines goes completely unrecognized until you see them in the proper light.

Astronomers discover stellar phenomena in a similar way. Innumerable bodies that are inconceivably far from our planet emit radiation all along the electromagnetic spectrum. One such body may not look particularly impressive when you're only looking at the radiation that the human eye can see—namely, visible light. But when astronomers use instruments to look at a different range of the spectrum and then convert it to a color that we recognize, suddenly the star can dazzle us with its beauty. There was far more coming out of it than we recognized at first!

In the same way, how we view anything complex rests heavily on the analytical tools we're using to look at it. Going with our gut is something like relying on our physical eyes under normal light conditions; we see something, but we don't see all there is to see.

This is how we commonly approach problems. We have a certain amount of wisdom from past experiences that we've saved in our mental bank, and we trot it out, consciously or not, to solve new problems that arise. But sometimes that's not enough, and we get stuck. Moreover, our experiential wisdom falls short of the riches God has provided to us in the gospel.

The gospel is sort of like the ultraviolet light bombarding those rocks from New Jersey or like the instruments that see all the radiation emitted by a star. It's a fresh, uniquely Christian, and (I would argue) comprehensive way of looking at the difficulties we face. By itself it doesn't provide all the detail that might be helpful, but it does enable us to make sense of our problems in a way that we couldn't otherwise. The gospel isn't just something we can look at; it's something we can use to look at everything else.

However, this isn't automatic or easy even if we're very familiar with the gospel. We still have to put together and set up the instrument and learn how to use it. This chapter describes how to use the gospel as a tool to analyze problems. In addition to my own ideas, I'm building on the work of others and trying to take it a step farther by integrating different models together into a coherent whole. So stay with me as I walk you through the complexity step by step, because we'll have a much more powerful instrument on the other side.

All the Problems in the World

The first way to analyze problems is simply to name them. Some people make bold claims that the gospel solves all our problems. I happen to agree with them. Yet if that's true, then it's necessary to define all the problems that we claim that the gospel solves.

When we run into a problem in life, it might be common and easily labeled—for example, "I lost my job." But that label obscures the complexity of the problem, because there are actually quite a number of simple, basic problems bundled into that one big one. These include problems having to do with the body and one's physical surroundings, with relationships, and with one's interior life in addition to problems having to do with work.

Moreover, even those basic problems—the ramifications of the big one—come in pairs. One half of the problem is what I call a *hurt*; it's the pain you have that you don't want. The other half of the problem I call a *craving*; it's the good that you want that you don't have.

To reveal the difficulties we face for what they are, we can analyze them according to the virtually comprehensive list of basic human problems in Table 1.

Table 1a – Physical Problems

Hurts	Cravings
Starvation	Satiation
Homelessness	Dwelling
Destitution	Possessions
Sickness	Health
Disability	Strength

Hurts	Cravings
Hardship	Comfort
Captivity	Liberty
Theft	Security
Violence	Safety
Sexual Frustration	Sexual Pleasure
Mortality	Immortality

Table 1b – Relationship Problems

Hurts	Cravings
Orphanhood	Parents
Being Unknown	Being Known
Exclusion	Belonging
Neglect	Attention
Loneliness	Companionship
Condemnation	Approval
Disrespect	Esteem
Rejection	Love
Deception	Truth-Telling
Betrayal	Faithfulness
Lovelessness	Romance
Group Inferiority	Group Honor

Table 1c – Mind Problems

Hurts	Cravings
Demonic Oppression	Cleansed Mind
Addiction	Self-Mastery
Terror	Calm
Despair	Hope
Guilt	Justification
Embarrassment	Dignity
Self-Loathing	Self-Esteem
Personal Unattractiveness	Personal Attractiveness
Chaos	Order
Ugly Surroundings	Beautiful Surroundings
Ignorance	Knowledge
Boredom	Delight
Loss	Permanence

Table 1d – Achievement Problems

Hurts	Cravings
Servitude	Freedom
Exploitation	Fairness

Hurts	Cravings
Uselessness	Being Needed
Pointlessness	Purpose
Fruitlessness	Accomplishment
Childlessness	Parenthood
Afflicted Child	Flourishing Child
Failure	Success
Defeat	Victory
Impotence	Power
Insignificance	Importance
Forced Conformity	Self-Expression

(Before moving on, is it just me, or do we humans have a lot of problems?)

How does this discouraging list help us address other people's needs with the gospel? Start by imagining that a friend of yours, someone you know personally, loses his job. You care about your friend and want to sympathize with him in a comforting way. However, even though you've had problems in life, you've never lost your job, so it's a little hard for you know how to relate. So you take a look at this list of problems and realize that your friend may be experiencing or threatened by any of these:

- Starvation (i.e., loss of satiation)

- Homelessness (loss of dwelling)

- Destitution (loss of possessions)

- Hardship (loss of comfort)

- Exclusion (loss of belonging)

- Loneliness (loss of companionship)

- Condemnation (loss of approval)

- Disrespect (loss of esteem)

- Rejection (loss of love)

- Terror (loss of calm)

- Despair (loss of hope)

- Guilt (loss of justification)

- Embarrassment (loss of dignity)

- Self-loathing (loss of self-esteem)

- Loss (loss of permanence)

- Uselessness (loss of being needed)

- Fruitlessness (loss of accomplishment)

- Failure (loss of success)

- Defeat (loss of victory)

- Impotence (loss of power)

- Insignificance (loss of importance)

This is an especially long list because losing a job is an especially traumatic and complex problem. Yet as you look at this list, you begin to see ways you can relate to your friend; just because you haven't lost a job doesn't mean that you haven't experienced many of these same basic problems in other situations. You also benefit from seeing the problems you *can't* relate to; you're able to respect the fact that you can't fully understand what he's going through, and you can name part of why that is.

As we imagine writing a word of gospel-based encouragement

to the unknown person who has just experienced job loss, it will help us to remember that for the gospel to solve their problem, it has to solve *each* of their problems. The question is, how does the word of God speak to everything in the whole range of difficulties that the person is experiencing? Obviously we can't shine a flashlight at every nook and cranny of the issue in one brief blog post. Nevertheless, looking at the problem this way can generate loads of ideas for writing (and preaching) that you would never have thought up if you were relying solely on instinct born of your personal experience.

The Four Movements of the Gospel

Our next steps in building our problem-analyzing instrument are to tie these basic human problems to two different, complementary models of the gospel.

The first model of the gospel is the four-movement symphony of *creation-fall-redemption-new creation*, the story of the world God made us to inhabit:

Creation – The Triune God made all things, invisible (spiritual) and visible (physical). God made human beings, male and female, in the image of the Triune God to represent and mimic God on this planet as cultivators, beautifiers, namers, rulers, and multipliers. Human beings had no guilt, shame, or fear between each other and between themselves and God.

Fall – Succumbing to the enticement of Satan (a rebellious archangel), humans sought to become like God in competition with him rather than as reflections of him. They wanted to go their own way. By rebelling—sinning— against the source of their life, they lost the immortality that could have been theirs. Guilt, shame, fear, and conflict entered human existence: between people, between people and nature, between people and their bodies, between people and their self-concepts, and above all between people and God. All subsequent people, compulsively and by nature, replicate this pattern by making substitute gods of created things. All human problems ultimately stem from it.

Redemption – God the Father sent God the Son to become human, to unite humanity and divinity into his one Person—Jesus of Nazareth, the Anointed One (Messiah, Christ). He became like humans in every way and experienced what we do in every way except that there was not a hint of sin or rebellion in him. By God's intent, humans killed him. His death was the stand-in for the death all humans deserve; by it God absorbed God's just anger against evil within God so that evil humans could receive total forgiveness—a verdict of not guilty—and become reconciled to him, adopted into the Father's family as his own children.

New creation – In his life, Jesus repeatedly healed the painful consequences of sin that humans suffer (such as sickness)—a foretaste of a new world. After his death he rose from the dead in a new body as the prototype of a new humanity. He returned to heaven and sent his Holy Spirit into his followers, who began transforming them into that new humanity by replacing their natural sinful tendencies and multiplying the sort of miracles that Jesus performed. Jesus will return to judge the world, removing all evil—and those spirits and humans who cling to it—to permanent destruction and establishing a gloriously perfect world for completely renewed people.

You can diagram these four movements in the shape of a checkmark: from *good* (creation) to *worse* (fall) to *better* (redemption) to *best* (new creation). I call redemption "better" and new creation "best" not because the atonement in Christ's blood is anything less than it needs to be—quite the contrary! I simply mean that any of us who is fully and finally reconciled to God now find ourselves in a wonderful, vastly improved position, yet we still experience problems in "this present evil age" (Gal. 1:4). For now we get delicious tastes of the new creation, but someday the whole thing will be ours, and that future situation will be "best."

Another way to contrast redemption and new creation as I'm using the terms is with the words "statement" and "substance." On the one hand, the gospel is the *statement* of our new relationship with God. It is the declaration that we are innocent despite our guilt, that our sins are forgiven, that the debt has been paid, that peace has been made, that we have been adopted into a new family and named as heirs. "On paper," so to speak, this redemption has been complete since Jesus entered the Most Holy Place in heaven to make atonement for us with his own blood.

On the other hand, the gospel is the *substance* of salvation. It is the lived reality that Satan cannot dominate us, that sin cannot enslave us, that the world cannot withstand us—the reality of health in place of sickness, joy in place of despair, belonging in place of alienation, power in place of weakness, life in place of death. This new creation is partly experienced now by the Holy Spirit and fully experienced when Jesus returns.

Therefore, our problems—our hurts and cravings—look different depending on the movement of the gospel-symphony (table 2):

- In **creation**, there were no hurts, and cravings were satisfied. This actually remains somewhat true today, though in a seriously compromised way. The vast majority of the time, the vast majority of people are not experiencing all hurts and cravings at once. Therefore, in some ways people are doing well (unhurt and satisfied). This is proof that the goodness of creation is still present to a significant extent.

- In *the Fall*, hurts came into being, and cravings began to go unsatisfied. Again, not all hurts and cravings all the time, but everyone is experiencing some of these at any given time.

- In *redemption*, hurts and cravings are overshadowed. The goodness of redemption is so good that the bad things don't seem as bad; they certainly no longer appear permanent. Redemption also untangles the cords of our hearts that are wrapped around cravings that we've worshiped as false gods, hoping they would save us. It puts hurts and cravings in their proper perspective and cuts them down to size.

- In *new creation*, hurts are healed, and cravings are maximally satisfied. That is, they are satisfied in a way that goes far beyond the best that Adam and Eve themselves ever experienced. Moreover, the joy of having a wound healed surpasses the ease of never having been wounded at all. By God's grace, people in Christ experience some of this even in this present age.

I'd like to show you how each of these four movements writes a solution to human problems with a different color of ink, yet they combine to make a rich whole. But to do that, we first need to look at a second model of the gospel.

Moralism and Relativism

Timothy Keller is fond of portraying the gospel as the third way between two inferior, natural, human solutions: moralism and relativism.[10]

Moralism is based on a certain presupposition about how the

Table 2 – Four Movements of the Gospel

Creation	Good		No hurts, cravings satisfied
Fall	Worse		Hurts present, cravings unsatisfied
Redemption		(Statement)	Hurts and cravings overshadowed
New Creation		(Substance)	Hurts healed, cravings maximally satisfied

world works: "God (or the Universe) is *fair* to all. Therefore, if I *follow the rules* I will escape what hurts and will satisfy or eliminate my cravings." Obviously, different people from different philosophies, traditions, and cultures will define the rules somewhat differently, but the common belief is that if you do the right thing, things will turn out all right.

Now, this is has some genuine truth to it, and our four-movement description of the gospel tells us why. The first movement of the gospel is *creation*. God created a good world that was truly fair. When Adam and Eve followed the rules, they did indeed escape what hurt and satisfy their cravings.

As I claimed before, vestiges of that creation still exist in the world today. Few people are suffering in literally every way all of the time. And when people do the right thing, things do go better in their lives than they would otherwise.

But our grasp of the gospel also tells us why moralism fails. The second movement of the gospel is the *Fall*. As a result the world isn't fair anymore—bad things do happen to good people. But also as a result of the Fall, there are no truly, fully, deeply good people; good people simply aren't good enough. Even if the world *was* totally fair, no one is actually following the right rules well enough to avoid painful consequences.

So moralists are trying to live in a world created by a just God (whom they may not acknowledge) where the human race never suffered the Fall. However, that's not the real world. Moralists resist facing this reality and keep trying to follow the rules better and better—or pointing the finger at those who don't—hoping to achieve happiness and meaning that way. But the futility of the effort throws many into bitterness and cynicism at the unfairness of life.

On the other hand, some moralists do accept the truth of the Fall and don't expect life to be fair. But truly accepting the Fall includes accepting that they have failed too, and they cannot throw off their guilt no matter how much they try to improve. Either way, the natural result is despair.

But some people don't take the moralists' road. Instead, they opt for relativism.

Relativism is also based on a presupposition about how the world works—in this case, "God (or the Universe) is *good* to all. Therefore, if I *follow my own path* I will escape what hurts and will satisfy or eliminate my cravings." From this point of view, there are no guidelines outside the desires and wisdom of an individual's heart. As long as a person follows their heart, things have a way of turning out okay. In effect, the universe nourishes all its children who look for sustenance, whatever diverse paths they take to find it, so long as they are true to themselves.

Once again, this is not a crazy idea. God truly is good to all, and the world he created reflected that. Originally, Adam and Eve did not have impulses that required discipline or restraint. They did what came naturally to them, whatever it was, and they did indeed live superlatively happy lives.

And again, vestiges of that world remain today. People still have instincts of what they want and need that point to what will satisfy them. They still recoil from things that will harm them. And individuals (and families and organizations and communities and societies and civilizations) do often have a path to follow that isn't for everyone, because it fits their uniqueness and no one else's.

But once again, the Fall ruined all. There was one thing in Eden that was off-limits, and our first parents violated the boundary. God is still good to us, but we also exposed ourselves to his fierce anger against evil. Thorns and thistles—opposition, futility—impede us everywhere. And both our desires and our wisdom are now corrupted, so we can't trust that what we think is best for us really is.

So relativists are trying to live in a world created by a good God (whom they may not acknowledge) where the human race never suffered the Fall. However, as with the moralists, that's not the real world. Relativists resist facing this reality and keep trying one path after another or stubbornly stick to their individual way despite all evidence that it isn't a good one. But this way of living becomes frustrating and may make relativists desperate.

Some relativists try to close their eyes to reality even further by adopting a philosophy that everything actually is (or is "beyond") good. They try to believe that salvation comes from accepting that the universe really is good despite countless indications to the contrary. But willful blindness is a tough act to pull off.

How the Gospel Solves Our Problems

The gospel agrees with moralism and relativism as to creation, but it is superior to both because it takes the Fall seriously. Like the moralist and the relativist, the person who lives according to the gospel has a presupposition about how the world works. But the gospel presupposition is: "The God of the universe is both more fair than I imagined and more good than I imagined. Therefore, to escape what hurts and satisfy my cravings, I will *follow Christ*." The gospel provides the solutions we need, because in addition to creation and the Fall, the gospel also involves *redemption* and *new creation*.

A moralist who discovers redemption learns that God is actually more fair than she realized. God is so fair that he can't let *any* failure go unpunished, regardless of a person's intentions or excuses or apologies or improvement. Not only that, but a moralist's staunch rule-keeping is as bad as her occasional rule-breaking, because it's an assertion of independence from God and a denial of what God says is her true condition. God is so fair that he cannot simply sweep these offenses under the rug; he must make someone pay. Yet God exacted the full price from his only Son so the moralist can be forgiven.

A relativist who discovers redemption learns that God is actually more good than she realized. God is so good that he would go to any lengths to ensure a happy ending for someone no matter how wayward her path. In fact, the relativist's trust that God is good to all is actually her problem, because instead of following that good God, she's been following her heart away from him while paying lip-service to him. God is so good that he will not allow her to run headlong away from his goodness without experiencing pain as a wake-up call. But God is also so good that he absorbed the greatest pain caused by the relativist in himself when he gave up his Son to the cross to bring her home.

Redemption is this reconciling atonement by the blood of Jesus. Yet we pay a price in the exchange as well: the price of being right. We must admit that God is so fair and so good and that we are so *un*fair and *un*good that Jesus had to die as the only way to fix our problem. Yet coming to belong to a God like that is so wonderful that our hurts, our cravings, and above all our pride pale in comparison.

That's where the new creation comes in. Moralists want a universe that's fair. God offers a kingdom that is more fair than anything anyone has ever seen—a state of perfect righteousness and justice. And part of the offer is that children of the kingdom become righteous themselves, truly "fair" in everything they think, say, and do.

Relativists want a universe that's good. God offers an eternal life that is more good than anything anyone has ever experienced—a new, harmonious nature where there is no more death or sickness or heartbreak. And people who gain that kind of life in themselves acquire a new nature, all of whose instincts and desires and beliefs are truly good and always lead to goodness, wherever the person wants to go.

The key to all of this is Jesus Christ, God who became a man and died for us. He took on what it means to be us so we could take on what it means to be him. If you are one with him, you have atonement and reconcilation. If you are one with him, you have a place in the kingdom and eternal life. If you are one with him, you have righteousness and goodness because he is righteousness and goodness personified. That is the gospel.

Table 3 – Moralism, Relativism, and the Gospel

Movement	Approach	Fairness and Goodness	What Works
Creation	Moralism (follow the rules)	The Universe is fair (moralism) / The Universe is good (relativism)	Moralism and relativism work
Fall	Relativism (follow your heart)	The Universe is not fair / The Universe is not good	Moralism and relativism don't work
Redemption		God is more fair than imagined / God is more good than imagined	Atonement and reconciliation work
New Creation	Gospel (follow Christ)	You and the universe will be more fair (just) than imagined / You and the universe will be more good (well) than imagined	The kingdom and eternal life work

Four Answers to Any Problem

We've taken a deep dive into the gospel to see how we can use it to analyze people's problems and offer a solution. So what have we learned? How does it all come together practically?

First, when we look at a human problem, we can specify all the problems bundled in it. They include hurts suffered and unsatisfied cravings of many kinds. We may opt to focus on just one of the sub-problems as we think through a gospel-shaped solution.

To any problem, the gospel provides four complementary answers that correspond to the four movements of creation, fall, redemption, and new creation. Ultimately Christ is the center, and without him, no answer works fully and finally. Yet these four gospel-answers can be phrased without Christ so as to slip under the reader's religious sensitivities as an implicit setup to the explicit gospel.

The first answer corresponds to creation. This answer agrees with the answers of any modern moralist ("follow the rules") or relativist ("follow your heart"). There is much worldly wisdom that produces good results if you practice it. Christians mustn't shy away from it; it's actually part of our gospel. The instruction is, **obey it.**

The second answer corresponds to the Fall. This answer is cold comfort, but it is also a healthy dose of realism. It is the reminder that life is not fair and the world is not good, and it won't get better in any complete or permanent way. Not only that, but the person with the problem is part of the problem. The person may have contributed to the problem they're currently facing, but if not, they've certainly contributed to other people's problems. The instruction is, **admit it.**

The third answer corresponds to redemption. This answer asserts that rescue comes from outside ourselves because we can't get ourselves out of our own mess. We're not strong enough; we need help from someone else. Help may come from someone who knows what we don't or can supply what we lack. It may even come from someone who forgives us when we confess our share of responsibility for the problem we're in. In any case, the instruction is, *receive it.*

The fourth answer corresponds to new creation. This answer is imaginative, mysterious, and non-rational. It appeals to the dreams nested in people's hearts and woven into our stories. It is the hint that there is a world beyond our world that we can one day reach or that this world doesn't have to be the way it is forever. It is the suggestion that we wouldn't be able to imagine permanent perfection unless it really existed somewhere. The instruction is, *seek it.*

In the next chapter, I'll show you an example of how to express these answers in a 21st-century neotract for not-yet-disciples of Jesus.

7

The Epistle to the Person with the Cheating Boyfriend (Maybe)

A Gospel-Shaped Neotract

When we think about Billy Graham's contribution to the Christian movement, the first image that comes to mind is Graham standing on a platform in a huge stadium preaching to thousands of people. We might also picture him huddling with a president in the private wing of the White House. A few especially learned readers might recall him speaking from the podium at the First International Congress on World Evangelization at Lausanne in 1974.

But during Graham's career, he communicated his message to the most people most frequently through a syndicated newspaper column. *My Answer*, written by Graham and his team, ran in papers across the country for decades. It still appears in newspapers today, over 60 years after it began, with excerpts drawn from Graham's writings. It may have been his vehicle of greatest impact.

My Answer was formatted like any advice column. Ordinary Americans who never met Graham in person wrote him letters with questions about their everyday struggles. Graham responded with biblical advice, always concluding with an invitation to trust in Christ.

Graham earned readers' respect and trust with his preaching and his appearances on television, and that made people eager to read his advice. But the dynamic worked the other way as well: Graham's accessible, sincere, useful advice increased readers' trust and comfort with him.

This dynamic is still possible today. Churches and Christian leaders still have an opportunity to write solid, gospel-shaped advice that gains the trust and comfort of readers and subtly shifts their posture toward faith in Christ. However, our medium is not the newspaper but the internet, especially social media.

The following is a sample of one way to employ this strategy in our day—picture it as a blog post shared on social media. After the post I'll break down how it is built on the principles I elucidated in the last two chapters.

✳✳✳

"Is My Boyfriend Cheating on Me?": 5 Answers

He's hiding his phone when you walk in. He shows up late for no good reason. When you ask, "Who's that?" he replies, "No one."

You're worried. You do a dozen little things to show him how important he is to you, but he doesn't notice or he keeps his distance.

So the question niggles at your mind and won't go away: *Is he cheating on me?* Here are five ways to deal with that question.

#1 - Question the question

The big problem with this question is that it has no good answer.

On the one hand, if he is cheating, it is better to know it, because you can't have a relationship without faithfulness and honesty. But betrayal is devastating and certainly not the answer you want, even if it's the truth you need to know.

On the other hand, let's say he's *not* cheating. How will you ever know that for sure?

Think about this before you hire a private investigator or do your own sleuthing. It's impossible to prove beyond a shadow of a doubt that something *isn't* happening. The best you can do is to find no proof that he is cheating; you can't prove that he isn't.

Where will that leave you? Quite possibly stuck with the same worry and suspicion you have now.

#2 - Ask a better question

"Is my boyfriend cheating on me?" is an important question. But maybe there's actually a better question: What is really bothering me?

For instance, maybe there are other lies in the relationship—lies that he has told you or maybe even lies that you've told him—that have put a cloud of mistrust over everything. Or maybe he isn't giving you the attention or esteem or love you hoped for. Or maybe the way he acts embarrasses you in the eyes of your family or friends.

Is something like this the worry behind your worry? You might make a lot more progress trying to solve that problem than trying to prove that he is or is not cheating on you.

Couples counseling helps many people learn effective ways to communicate their fears and needs to their partner, and it provides a safe space to do it in. Alternatively, if trust has been badly compromised between you, you can always end the relationship.

But at the point of breaking it off, many people balk, even in cases where there's been one dishonesty after another. That's because "What is really bothering me?" can have an even deeper answer.

#3 - Look deep down

We're all missing something inside. You might call it confidence or maybe self-worth. Whatever you call what we're missing, it produces an uneasy sense that we're not right somehow.

Everyone uses strategies to fix this unease or cover it up both to others and to themselves. A very common strategy is to gain someone else's undying, completely accepting, perfectly faithful love.

Behind this strategy, deep down in places in our soul where we don't often go, might lurk beliefs like these:

- "If a man loves me, I'll know I'm worth loving."

- "If a man wants me, I'll know I'm beautiful."

- "If I stick by a man no matter what, I'll know I'm a good person."

If these beliefs came to the surface of our minds, we might blow them off. If we knew a friend believed them, we'd try to talk them out of it. But if these beliefs are inside us, they can powerfully affect our moods, attitudes, and actions.

#4 – Own your demands

Pretend for a second that you had one of these beliefs inside you. Can you imagine the pressure that would put on the man in your life? If he failed to love you perfectly (as you perceive it), your lovableness and worthiness would immediately be threatened. Preserving your self-worth is a heavy burden for him to carry. (And by the way, you might be carrying the same burden for *him*.)

The truth is, *no one* can carry that burden. Every person is unfaithful. Not all to the point of cheating with someone else, to be sure, but no one is perfectly, consistently loving. For example, there's never been a married person who has followed through on "to love and to cherish" every moment of every day.

So in this world as we know it, you can't avoid insecurity in relationships. If your self-worth is riding on it, it's going to be a very bumpy ride.

If there are problems in your relationship with your boyfriend, maybe this is your contribution to them. Maybe it would do your relationship good if you admitted it to him. This isn't about you taking responsibility for his unfaithful choices—that's all on him. It's right for you to demand faithfulness and honesty. But maybe you've been demanding something more than that: that he fill an emptiness deep within you that he can't fill.

#5 – Chase the story

Some people try to fill the hole inside with positive self-talk, but it only goes so far. We somehow know that we need an outside voice to affirm that we're good, yet no outside voice fits the bill.

Even so, something within us believes that that person exists. Otherwise, where do our stories come from? We have mountains of books and movies that depict the faithful lover who makes the main character's life complete. Where did the human race come up with the idea of this person we've never met?

But what if we did meet him, and we're trying to find him again? People in our church have come to believe that that's what happened. They say that the lover human beings once met is God. They say that coming back to God again—meeting him as a real person, more than an idea or a force or an imaginary friend—has started filling the hole in their lives that no one else could.

Whether that's your conclusion or not, maybe the best thing you can do now is to seek that lover who will never let you down—not in a boyfriend or even in yourself, but in something bigger and bolder than a human love can give.

✳✳✳

Let's analyze the construction of this sample blog post. First, let's look at the structure:

1. It's **1,000 words long**, which is the longest you want to go for this kind of post unless you have acquired a loyal following who will read anything you write.

2. It's formatted with **numbered headers** and little text in between. This allows people to skim the piece more easily if they're trying to evaluate quickly whether it's worth their time. It also keeps people engaged, because readers often hit the eject button when there's too much unbroken text (unless they're intentionally looking for that style, such as when reading long-form journalism on a topic of interest).

3. The numbered outline is also reflected in the **subtitle**, which is a standard hook for readers online. "5 Answers" communicates, "You can set your expectations for how long this is going to take." It also suggests that even if only one of the points proves to be worth the click, it's still a win for the reader.

4. The **title** is straight-up felt needs. Relationship issues are perhaps the biggest concerns in people's lives, and this is a classic one. It's worded for a specific target too. Could it be widened to "boyfriend or girlfriend"? Sure. Does it apply to married couples as well? Of course. But people don't search for solutions to problems in general. They search for solutions to their *specific* problem. Generic does not get found and does not get clicked—specific does.

5. Also note that the piece is written with an unmarried, coupled woman in mind as the **target reader**. But there is nothing in the piece that defines the reader outright, which allows a gay man to read it without bumping into an indicator that the advice is not for him.

Now let's look at the substance.

For this hypothetical situation, I decided to make *betrayal/faithfulness* the hurt-craving pair to focus on. I used the word "betrayal" once and cognates of "faithful" six times. (Notice the tilt toward the positive word of the pair, which affirms the reader's needs rather than drawing attention to their pain.)

Nevertheless, I also worked in other hurt-craving pairs that are pertinent to the situation. Under heading "#2" I asked, "What is really bothering me?" The following paragraph quickly ticks off possibilities: *deception/truth-telling, neglect/attention, disrespect/esteem, rejection/love,* and *embarrassment/dignity.* More pairs appear under "#3," shifting to an even deeper and more sensitive area of the soul: *self-loathing/self-esteem, attractiveness/unattractiveness,* and *guilt/justification*. All these help the reader think through their own situation, but they also may help the reader feel understood: *this author understands what I'm going through.*

All four movements of the gospel are reflected in the piece and shape the flow of thought:

- **Creation** appears in the consistent validation of the reader's expectation that their lover be faithful. It also undergirds the logical consideration of what might happen as a result of investigating unfaithfulness. (Remember, Jesus is the "Logos" through whom God created the world [John 1:1-3]; creation is logical.) Creation is also implicit in the advice to enter couples counseling, and thus to be exposed to wisdom (another key element of creation—Prov. 8).

- The **Fall** appears when the piece examines the reader's inner emptiness and unease, when it suggests that the reader's own demands may have contributed to their problem, and when it points out that no person is perfectly faithful or can meet our need.

- **Redemption** appears in the suggestion that the reader might confess to their boyfriend that they've been demanding more than he can deliver as a step toward reconciliation.

- **New creation** appears when the reader is prompted to consider where the universal idea of the perfect lover comes from. It closely follows C. S. Lewis's "argument from desire": "If I find in myself a desire which no experience in this world can satisfy, the most probable explanation is that I was made for another world."[11]

This last passage is the only point where God is brought up in the piece, not as a truth-claim but simply as something that people in our community believe. The third person—"they," not "we"—is less direct and potentially threatening than a first-person wording. It presents God—specifically as we have found him—simply as an option to consider. Nevertheless, the final call to action urges the reader to intensify their search and to raise it above the human plane. It endeavors to strengthen the longing within the reader and their dissatisfaction with this world in hope that they will eventually lead the reader to Christ.

This piece doesn't assume the general knowledge of or respect for the Bible that Billy Graham's advice columns did in the last century. It tilts toward pre-evangelism, but it is an evangelistic piece all the same. Even though the gospel is not explicit in it, the whole piece is shaped by it. Appreciating this piece is a step toward embracing the gospel that the reader doesn't know they are taking—especially when they take that step in the context of a relationship with the Christian friend who shared it with them.

8

Start Now

Two Ways to Make Killer Content from What You're Already Doing

From "Show Up" to "Grow Up" was written to expose and explode the default model of church communications that rests on the default model of discipleship—namely, program attendance. More than that, this book was written to open eyes to the possibility of a new evangelistic communication tool for the 21st century, the "neotract." We re-examined the gospel we proclaim, and we looked at a prototype of a fresh way to connect it to the everyday problems of everyday people.

To conclude, I want to describe two other practical vehicles for presenting the gospel in a church's outbound communication.

Sermon Rechanneling

First, if you haven't realized it yet, everything I write about gospel-shaped solutions to common human problems can be applied to preaching. The preached word in the assembly of the believers should be much more explicit about Christ than the neotract blog post presented in the last chapter. Nevertheless, the same principles apply. The dichotomy between "felt-needs" preaching and "gospel-centered" preaching is a false choice. (Oh, how the devil loves false choices!) Perhaps the most powerful preaching in this era—perhaps in any era—is preaching that provides a solution to people's felt needs that is deeply gospel-shaped, not "gospel-slapped."

But once you've preached that magnificent, gospel-centered felt-needs sermon, then what do you do with it?

Many churches record sermon video and upload it to YouTube or their website. Many also convert the audio into a podcast episode. These are great moves, and if you're doing them, keep it up.

But churches are still missing a golden opportunity to rechannel the sermon content into text. I'm not talking about a transcript of the whole sermon (and certainly not the notes). I'm talking about converting sermons into neotracts.

Depending on the preacher, a single sermon could yield one to three blog posts. These can be retooled for a different target audience than the one you preached the message to—namely, the unbeliever who won't (yet) come to your church instead of the unbeliever who decided to give it a try.

Importantly, these repackaged written adaptations of your oral sermon ought to be snack-sized. Somebody has to be very word-hungry to consume an entire sermon in audio or video form. But almost anyone has time to nibble on a 1,000-word article, at least to glance at its section headings. With a neotract, the barrier to engagement is far lower than a full-length message.

Anchor E-book

For the second gospel vehicle, do you have that book you want to write? The one you have a table of contents for but haven't started yet? The opportunity to reach people with the gospel week in and week out might be the motivation that gets you to write it for real . . . or it gets you to ask for help from someone who can turn your spoken words into written ones.

Even if writing a book hasn't been your dream, if you're a preacher, you are creating fresh content all the time. The church is a content factory. Its problem isn't that it doesn't have anything to say; its problem is that it isn't maximizing the delivery of what it does say. One way to maximize content is to view your next gospel-centered and felt-needsy sermon series as an e-book waiting to be written.

Self-publishing options abound, from Amazon's Kindle Direct Publishing to the expedient of saving a document in EPUB format or PDF and posting it on your website. But it doesn't stop there. Once you publish your e-book, you can spend weeks drawing excerpts out of it and shaping them into shareable, snackable blog posts for the reader who won't (yet) commit to reading the whole thing.

Get Started

So now what do I do? I'm glad you asked.

Here's your four-point punch list to rebalance your church's outbound communication from a steady diet of "show up" back towards "grow up." Do the ones you're eager to do and get partners to do the ones that aren't in your wheelhouse:

- Put a blog page on your website. Don't have a website? Jump onto a site like Wix or Squarespace and make one now while you wait for a professionally designed site later. (Do you or someone in your church take pictures of events, people, or the building? You'll want those.)

- Are you preaching this week? Consider: what felt need does your passage or topic address? Craft a gospel-shaped response.

- Convert the sermon into one or more neotracts and post one this week.

- Recruit at least ten people to share the blog post on their social media feeds. (Also put it on the church's social media feeds.) Explain the evangelistic use of the post; make sure they understand that the goal of sharing is to start meaningful conversations between them and their friends, online or offline, and to lay the track for a later invitation to church. Do you have staff? Make sharing the post a part of their job description unless they give you a really good reason not to.

A Final Word

Before you get started on your way, let me give you one last word of encouragement.

Remember, the Master who called you never gave you the assignment of getting people to show up. That assignment came from someone else, somewhere else. His assignment to you was to make disciples of the "crowd" that has already shown up all around you.

What is more, he promised that he himself has already shown up to grow you: "I am with you always, to the end of the age" (Matt. 28:20). Together with others as parts of Jesus' one body, you can proclaim his gospel to all creation. He is with you.

ACKNOWLEDGMENTS

I would like to thank a few people for how they helped me form the ideas of From "Show Up" to "Grow Up" or make it available to the wider public.

I first want to thank Richard Fink, who designed the cover of this book and the images that appeared on social media advertising it. Richard devoted remarkable creativity, thoughtfulness, craftsmanship, and communication with me to make it just right.

The thoughts I expressed in this work were influenced by multiple sources that to some degree are reflected in the notes at the end of this book. Yet I would specifically like to credit Bobby Warrenburg for asking me questions and sharing with me thoughts and material (notably an unpublished essay by Tim Keller) that impelled me to think more comprehensively than ever before about how exactly the gospel is the answer to our questions and the solution to our problems.

Will Mancini is not only a client I am honored to serve at Fulcrum Content; he is a partner, a mentor, and a dear friend and brother. His influence seeps into me in ways known and unknown, and his generous spirit in all manner of ways blows across these pages.

Since this is the first publication of Fulcrum Content, I want to honor Matt Paonessa of JMG Systems, who inspired the launch of this enterprise and gave it critical support as a fledgling company.

Lastly, I cannot write a book without acknowledging my wife Kelly, my biggest fan.

NOTES

[1] Carey Nieuwhof, "10 Predictions About The Future Church and Shifting Attendance Patterns," https://careynieuwhof.com/10-predictions-about-the-future-church-and-shifting-attendance-patterns (accessed August 9, 2018).

[2] James Emery White, *The Rise of the Nones: Understanding and Reaching the Religiously Unaffiliated* (Grand Rapids, MI: Baker Books, 2014).

[3] I'm indebted to Finney scholar Garth Rosell for this interpretation of Finney's teaching.

[4] William Safire, "On Language: The Elision Fields," *New York Times*, August 13, 1989, SM18; quoted in "Showing Up Is 80 Percent of Life," Quote Investigator, https://quoteinvestigator.com/2013/06/10/showing-up (accessed August 13, 2018).

[5] Bobby Harrington and Greg Wiens, *Becoming a Disciple Maker: The Pursuit of Level 5 Disciple Making.* Available for download at https://discipleship.org/ebooks/becoming-a-disciple-maker and https://exponential.org/resource-ebooks/disciplemaking (as of September 18, 2018). Harrington and Wiens' schema builds on the one expounded by Harrington and Josh Patrick in their book *The Disciple Maker's Handbook* (Grand Rapids, MI: Zondervan, 2017).

[6] See, for example, John 7:49, where the chief priests and Pharisees say, "This crowd that does not know the law is accursed" (ESV). The NIV translates the term with "mob" and the NET with "rabble."

[7] Without going into detail, the big indicators come from comparing John to the Synoptic Gospels (Matthew, Mark, and Luke) as well as looking more carefully at the sequence in the Synoptics themselves. This examination seems to indicate multiple callings of some of the same disciples to progressively greater levels of commitment; an extended period of ministry centered in Judea (described in John) before the period centered in Galilee began (where almost all the plot of the Synoptics takes place); and multiple festivals in Jerusalem attended by Jesus and named in John that stretched over many months.

[8] "When he saw the crowds, he went up the mountain. After he sat down his disciples came to him. Then he began to teach them" (Matt. 5:1-2).

[9] *Torah* is Hebrew for "an instruction." Jews a century or two before Jesus, when translating *torah* into Greek, used the word for "law." As a proper noun, the Torah is the collection of instructions that Moses received from God. "Torah" became the favored term for the first five books of the Bible, which contain those instructions. The Pharisees, however, also believed in an oral Torah that Moses did not write down but was passed down the centuries to their day. Jesus denied that those oral regulations and interpretations were actually Torah from God; he dismissed them as "human tradition" (Mark 7:6-13). That disagreement was one of the biggest causes of conflict between Jesus and the Pharisees.

[10] Tim Keller, "The Centrality of the Gospel," unpublished essay.

[11] C. S. Lewis, *Mere Christianity* (San Francisco: Harper San Francisco Publishers, 2001), 136-137.

ABOUT THE AUTHOR

Cory Hartman is the founder and principal writer at Fulcrum Content, the company he launched to equip churches for disciple-making and help leaders extend their reach with the written word. At Fulcrum, Cory serves as a collaborative author for thought-leaders, provides editing and self-publishing assistance, writes original online pieces, adapts audio and video content into engaging articles, writes marketing copy, and crafts custom-built discipleship material.

Cory served as a pastor for 13 years in churches in Pennsylvania and New Jersey. He earned a doctor of ministry degree from Gordon-Conwell Theological Seminary with a thesis on 19th-century educator, revivalist, publisher, and abolitionist Mansfield French. Cory previously earned an MDiv from Gordon-Conwell in urban ministry and a BA from Taylor University in biblical literature (church music minor).

Cory's letters have appeared in such publications as the *Boston Globe* and the *Newark Star-Ledger*, the latter winning the paper's Silver Pen Award. He the author of *On Freedom and Destiny: How God's Will and Yours Intersect*. One of his most enjoyable personal accomplishments is to have been a one-day champion on the TV quiz show *Jeopardy!*

A native of central New York State, Cory's family roots are in central Pennsylvania, where he now lives with his wife Kelly and their four children.

Made in the USA
Lexington, KY
22 July 2019